By 1963 many BET operators had tried rear-engine double-deckers, but had then reverted to traditional front-engine types. Prior to receiving its first Atlanteans in the years 1960-62, Western Welsh had purchased AEC Regent Vs and Bridgemasters. In 1963 it received ten forward-entrance Regent Vs with Northern Counties bodies, followed by 21 Leyland PD2A/27 models with 65-seat Weymann bodywork to a similar layout. They were numbered 900-20 (900-20 DBO) and were not particularly attractive buses compared to the Regent Vs. These were the last new Leyland PD2s for a BET operator, no others having been received since 1957 when BET turned to the longer PD3 in large numbers. In August 1974 the whole batch was renumbered H11-3163 and on 26 April 1978, twelve of these Leyland Titans transferred to National Welsh. H1963 (908 DBO) was amongst them and is seen the following day on a school service at Stanwell Road, Penarth. It was one of five allocated to Penarth Road, Cardiff, depot at this time and was withdrawn later the same year.

*(Paul Dudley)*

1

Control of the much-loved Neath & Cardiff Luxury Coaches (N&C) passed to South Wales Transport in April 1969 but retained its identity a little longer. On 1 January 1971 the NBC disbanded the Neath & Cardiff fleet, and Western Welsh received six former N&C coaches, together with a share in the express route from Swansea to Cardiff. The coaches were all AEC Reliances and included bodywork by Harrington, Duple, Northern, and Plaxton. Just two survived long enough to pass into National Welsh ownership, UD4368 (PTX 830F) and UC4469

(UNY 831G). UD4368, fitted with a Plaxton Panorama body seating 41, is seen in Cardiff bus station on 28 May 1978. It had been downgraded to dual-purpose specification in April 1974 by converting the door to power operation, and fitting out the vehicle for one-person operation. UD4368 was withdrawn in August 1979 and passed to a local enthusiast for preservation. He still owned the vehicle in 2019, based at the Barry depot of the Cardiff Transport Preservation Group.

*(Paul Dudley)*

James of Ammanford and Maidstone and District were early customers for the Weymann-bodied semi-lowbridge Leyland Atlantean, and Western Welsh received its first twelve examples in January and February 1960, numbered 301-12. The low-height bodies featured an awkward raised seating area at the rear of the upper saloon, which barely provided sufficient headroom in the rear portion of the lower saloon. They were popular with staff and passengers alike, but were not without reliability issues, particularly early on. Just two years later and Western Welsh had a total of 66 examples in service across South Wales with Cardiff, Barry and Bridgend garages having substantial allocations. By August 1974 349 (349 ABO) had gained NBC poppy red livery and had become LR1862. Just half a dozen of this type passed to National Welsh in April 1978 for further service though LR1862 was not amongst them. It had been taken out of service in January despite receiving National Welsh fleet names as seen here at Barry depot on 29 April 1978.

*(Paul Dudley)*

This shot was taken in the yard at Penarth Road depot, Cardiff, on 22 July 1978. It shows H11/9/2563 (900/8/14 DBO), three of the Weymann-bodied Leyland PD2As that passed to National Welsh three months earlier. Two of them lacked destination blinds, and may well have been withdrawn from service by this time. As mentioned on page 1, this batch originally comprised 21 buses that were based at Cardiff, Barry and Bridgend depots. A number of them transferred to Porth depot after 1971, and during 1975, six of them received NBC-style Rhondda fleet names. The first two examples were withdrawn in the autumn of 1975, when H2363 (912 DBO) was cannibalised while H2863 (917 DBO) was sold for further service. Returning to this view, H11/963 were sold for scrap in 1979, while H2563 continued in service until the following year when the seven surviving PD2As were taken out of service.

*(Paul Dudley)*

The National Eisteddfod was held in Cardiff between 7 and 12 August 1978 when a special service numbered 51 was operated between Llandaff Fields, Castle Street, Newport Road, Waterloo Road and the Eisteddfod field at Pentwyn. The licence was taken out by City of Cardiff Transport but the operation of the vehicles and drivers was sub-contracted to National Welsh and Taff-Ely Borough Council. National Welsh supplied a number of Leyland Nationals including a well turned-out N4177 (SKG 914S) which was an 11.3-metre 49-seat model.

It had been delivered in late 1977 and entered service in January 1978, and was one of a batch of eighteen similar buses new around this time. N4177 was renumbered N1604 in January 1983 and was by then working from National Welsh's Ross-on-Wye garage, which of course was in England. It received Red & White fleet names in October 1984 and became N604 in the February 1986 fleet renumbering.

*(the late John Wiltshire)*

We are in the upper Rhondda Fawr valley on 2 September 1978 for this view of Northern Counties-bodied Leyland Atlantean HR3769 (VTG 511G). The bus is working to Porth with the 11.43 departure from Blaencwm, a small former mining community at the head of the valley. It is making its way towards Treherbert along St. Albans Terrace, Tynewydd. For many years Rhondda Transport standardised on the AEC Regent V for its double deck requirements taking its last examples in 1966. Unlike neighbouring former BET fleet Western Welsh, which had received its first Atlanteans in 1960, the first Rhondda Atlanteans did not arrive until September 1968. 496–501, fitted with 73-seat Northern Counties bodywork, were followed by a further ten similar buses (502-11) in July 1969, and all sixteen passed to Western Welsh on 1 January 1971. They were renumbered HR1-668 and HR1-1069 in 1974 and then HR44-968 and HR28-3769 in 1975. Having passed to National Welsh ownership in April 1978, HR3769 was withdrawn in 1980 and sold to a dealer.

*(Geoff Gould)*

In 1962 Western Welsh received eighteen Willowbrook-bodied Leyland Leopards numbered 601-18 (601-18 BBO). These were the company's first Leopards and first 36-foot long vehicles and had an impressive seating capacity of 54. When new, twelve of them were allocated to Bridgend depot for use on services in the Llynfi, Ogmore and Garw valleys. 612 passed to South Wales Transport in March 1972 with the transfer of the Haverfordwest depot and services. The others were renumbered U13-2962 in 1974 and then U48-6462 in October 1975. It would appear that only eight remained in service upon the creation of National Welsh in April 1978, largely shared between Bridgend, Barry and Crosskeys depots. However this view taken at Tonypandy on 2 September 1978 would indicate that U5962 (613 BBO) may be working from Porth depot. It is seen in Dunraven Street with the 13.28 service from Blaenrhondda.

*(Geoff Gould)*

Rhondda Transport favoured the Leyland Tiger Cub for many years, not taking its first Leopards until April 1968. On order for 1971, Rhondda had ten PSU4A/2R models with 45-seat Willowbrook bodies and these were delivered to Western Welsh in full Rhondda livery as 2325-34 in April that year. They remained based at Porth depot, and were to be found working a wide variety of routes. They were renumbered U11-2071 in 1974, passing to National Welsh in April 1978. U1271 (BTX 326J) is noted on Cymmer Hill, Trebanog Road, on 2 September 1978. At this time the 509 ran between Porth (Upper Gynor Place) and Tonyrefail. U1271 was withdrawn in late 1983, and two of this batch later became towing buses for National Welsh including BTX 332J which survives in preservation.

*(Geoff Gould)*

On 1 October 1978, having departed Merthyr Tydfil bus station, RD5968 (OAX 3F) is about to turn out of Castle Street onto Merthyr's ring road. It will cross the River Taff before climbing out of the town and descending into the Cynon Valley at Hirwaun. Its destination blind still proudly displays its ancestry as one of 32 similar ECW coach-bodied Bristol RELH received by Red & White between 1966 and 1969. RD5968 was delivered in cream and red livery in February 1968 as RC368 and would later receive corporate overall white NBC coach livery. It was renumbered RC5968 in October 1975, and then RD5968 in September 1976 when it was demoted to a dual-purpose vehicle with the appropriate NBC livery which suits the vehicle quite well. RD5968 was withdrawn in late 1982 though was allocated new fleet number RD1331 in January 1983. It seems unlikely that it ever carried this number, and it was sold to a Barnsley area breaker in September the same year.

*(John Jones)*

U4168 (RTG 320F) is arriving at Newport on the afternoon of Saturday 28 October 1978 having worked into town on the 123 service from Blaenavon. U4168 is a Leyland Leopard PSU3/2R with a Willowbrook DP49F body, the middle one of three new to Rhondda Transport in the spring of 1968. Equipped for one person operation from new, they passed into the Western Welsh fleet on 1 January 1971 as 2319 to 2321, and remained at Porth depot. 2320 received the standard NBC dual-purpose bus livery in 1973, and was renumbered UD568 in August 1974. It then became UD4168 in October 1975, and all three Leopards were downgraded to buses duties in January 1977. UD4168 then became U4168 and was transferred to Crosskeys depot, but had moved to Cwmbran by the end of that year. In January 1978 it gained bus seats and was repainted into NBC bus livery as seen in this view. The bus was withdrawn and sold in December 1980.

*(John Jones)*

The Rhondda Transport Co Ltd received its first Leyland Tiger Cubs in 1953 and, apart from three Bedford coaches, the type reigned supreme for fifteen years, a fleet of 84 having been amassed when the last examples were received in 1968. These were numbered 304 to 318 (RTG 304-18F) and were fitted with BET-style Marshall bodywork. The final three were 41-seat dual-purpose vehicles, the remainder being 45-seat buses; all were equipped for one-person operation.

Numbered 2304-18 by Western Welsh in 1971, they received Red & White style fleet numbers U2-1368 and UD1-368 three years later. To complicate matters, in October 1975 they were renumbered to U21-3268 and UD37-968. On 19 June 1979, U2468 (RTG 307F) is seen high above Risca on Manor Way, Ty-Sign, with a 154 service to Cardiff. U2468 was withdrawn in 1980, and together with the rest of this batch, was sold to a dealer.

*(Geoff Gould)*

In 1960 Red & White received twenty Bristol Lodekkas of the less common FL6G variety. These 30-foot double-deckers were numbered L1-260 (VAX 508/9, 3-20 AAX), and 70-seat ECW bodies fitted with platform doors. Six of them passed to National Welsh in April 1978, including two that were in use as training vehicles. One of those still in normal service was L1360 (13 AAX) which dated from October 1960 and is seen here, in excellent condition, at Markham on 22 June 1979 working a Crosskeys College to Tredegar service. The bus was withdrawn shortly afterwards and was repainted canary yellow as driver training bus T6 where it joined T1 (20 AAX) and T2 (5 AAX). It was later renumbered T1068 and was sold for scrap in August 1985.

*(Geoff Gould)*

National Welsh inherited thirteen former Western Welsh AEC Renowns with Northern Counties bodywork in April 1978. They were distributed between Barry and Cwmbran depots together with a solitary example at Crosskeys. The oldest of these was L3764 (BKG 713B) which had been new as Western Welsh 713 in October 1964. Its claim to fame was that it had been exhibited at the 1964 Commercial Motor Show, and was also the first AEC Renown to be bodied by the Wigan coachbuilder. Western Welsh had 28 Renowns numbered 713-740, and they were the last new half-cabs for this operator. In January 1972 four of them, together with Neath depot and its services, passed to South Wales Transport. 713 was renumbered L164 in 1974 and then L3764 in October 1975. On 16 June 1979 it is parked at Cwmbran depot with similar L6565 (BKG 722C) and L5166 (HKG 732D) for company. L3764 was the last AEC Renown in service with National Welsh, and was sold for preservation in January 1981.

*(Geoff Gould)*

From its creation in April 1978, National Welsh's area of operation could be summed up as south-east Wales, south Herefordshire and the Forest of Dean area of Gloucestershire. R4865 (GAX 1C) was numerically the first of eleven Bristol RELL6G saloons delivered to Red & White in the autumn of 1965 and originally numbered R1-1165. They had 54-seat ECW bodywork and were the first rear-engine vehicles for the company. R165 (GAX 1C) entered service from Chepstow depot and later transferred to Cinderford. Many of this batch spent much of their working lives based in Monmouthshire and the Forest of Dean, and they became R48-5875 in October 1975. Withdrawals commenced in 1978 with the demise of R52/865 (GAX 5/11C), of which GAX 11C went for further service. The last two went in 1980, including R4865 (GAX 1C) which bowed out in February after service at Abergavenny depot, which is where this photograph was taken.

*(Cliff Essex)*

Western Welsh was an early customer for the Leyland Atlantean before returning to front-engine AEC Regent Vs, Leyland PD2As and finally AEC Renowns. When Leyland developed an Atlantean with a drop-centre rear axle which allowed a normal seating layout within low-height bodywork, Western Welsh received ten with Northern Counties bodies, numbered 367-376, in 1969. Of these, 367 and 374-6 were latterly based at Haverfordwest depot and consequently passed to South Wales Transport in 1972. The remainder were renumbered LR1-669 in 1974 and LR22-769 in 1975, while the four with South Wales Transport returned east in March/April 1979 to become National Welsh LR56-969. LR5769 and LR5969 were initially based at Cinderford in the Forest of Dean and on 4 July 1979, LR5769 (PKG 374H) stands in glorious late evening Gloucestershire sunshine at Huntley while working from Gloucester to Cinderford.

*(Geoff Gould)*

Rhondda Transport had been an enthusiastic AEC Regent buyer since 1933, and continued to receive them almost to the end of production. Of 98 AEC Regent Vs delivered between 1956 and 1966, the first 27 had exposed radiators and open rear platform bodywork by Weymann. All that followed were to forward-entrance layout, initially on 30-foot chassis, but from 1962, on 27-foot medium-weight chassis with AV470 engines. The final 27 Regent Vs, numbered 469 to 495 were the 2MD3RA air-braked model with attractive and well-appointed 65-seat Northern Counties bodies, and compared very favourably with the spartan Metro-Cammell and Weymann bodies of earlier deliveries. All 27 passed to Western Welsh on 1 January 1971 retaining their Rhondda fleet numbers, and in August 1974 they became H1-1064, H1-1265 and H1-566. Some had left the fleet before the October 1975 renumbering, though H865 (ETX 486C) did become H7965 and is seen here at Dinas between Porth and Penygraig in June 1979. This bus was one of the last three remaining Regent Vs when withdrawal came in 1979.

*(Peter Smith)*

From 1953, over a period of fourteen years Western Welsh received 349 Leyland Tiger Cubs. For 1965 there were 41 Park Royal-bodied examples numbered 1334 to 1348, with 41 high-backed seats and 1349 to 1374, with 43 bus seats, although ten of them did not enter service until 1966 and received D-suffix registrations. In 1972 six of them passed to South Wales Transport together with Western Welsh's Haverfordwest and Neath garages, while a further six passed to Crosville Motor Services with the garages at Newquay and Newcastle Emlyn. FUH 362D was new in January 1966 as 1362 and was renumbered U1966 in 1974, latterly based at Cwmbran depot. It was withdrawn in 1980 and became a temporary towing vehicle as seen entering Newport bus station on 3 May 1980.

*(John Jones)*

Red & White Services Ltd received 202 Bristol MWs between 1957 and 1966; the first sixteen were MW5Gs while the remainder, including all 51 coaches, were MW6Gs. 16 FAX, a 45-seat bus, was one of the batch numbered U1-1262 (11-22 FAX) and entered service from Aberdare depot in February 1963. U662 was working from Monmouth by September 1969 and received NBC poppy red livery in November 1972. In October 1975 it was renumbered U4162 and passed to Western Welsh in January 1978, but was not used. It remained sidelined by National Welsh until it became training bus T5 in July 1979. Strangely, and despite its new role, in this view at Aberdare depot in September 1979, it appears to have received a full repaint in service livery including its old number. It was later renumbered T1067, before passing to a dealer for scrap in 1985.

*(Peter Smith)*

The second delivery of Bristol RELL buses to Red & White arrived in 1967 and comprised five vehicles, R1-567 with 50 high-backed seats in ECW bus bodies for use on the Cardiff – Bristol services 300 and 301. Unlike the RELLs new in 1965, these vehicles were fitted with Leyland engines and semi-automatic transmission. They featured the revised style of body with peaked roof domes and a flat two-piece windscreen. There followed in 1968 a further twenty similar vehicles, R1-2068 (RAX 1-20G) but with 53 ordinary bus seats. On 3 May 1980

Tredegar-based R768 (RAX 7G) is seen racing towards Caerphilly on the A468 between Rhiwderin and Lower Machen. It is working the 150 from Newport to Merthyr Tydfil which, at this time, was jointly operated with Rhymney Valley District Council. The shallow two-piece windscreen is clearly evident in this view as it passes under the bridge which still carries an operational railway line to Machen Quarry. Most of this batch was taken out of service in 1980 though five soldiered on long enough to be renumbered in 1983.

*(John Jones)*

15

LR8010 (BUH 238V) is a Bristol VRT/SL3/501 fitted with a standard 74-seat ECW body, built to the lowest available overall height of 13ft 5in. It was one of ten similar buses numbered LR8001-10 received in January/February 1980 that were to have originally been numbered LR41-5079. From 1980, all additions to the National Welsh fleet received fleet numbers with the year of manufacture given first. Four buses from this batch, including LR8010 were initially allocated to Tredegar depot, and in this view it is seen leaving Castle Street, Merthyr Tydfil, on 11 May 1980, working the 156 to Newport via Tredegar, Blackwood and Crosskeys. This bus became LR1713 in 1983, and moved to Bridgend depot in 1985. In early 1986 it was renumbered LD713 after receiving 67 coach-type seats. It was withdrawn in 1992 and passed to Morris Travel of Pencoed. BUH 238V moved on to a preservationist in 2004, but was unfortunately broken up in 2012.

*(John Jones)*

Red & White's second batch of Bristol RE buses comprised 21 Series 1 RESL models with Leyland engines and semi-automatic gearboxes. Numbered RS1-2167, they were some of the last to carry the original well-rounded style of ECW bodywork and were all based at Aberdare garage where most spent their entire working lives. In October 1975 these extremely popular buses were renumbered RS29-4967. The photographer has caught RS4767 (LAX 119E), complete with Cynon-Dare local identity branding, in the bus station at Pontypridd on 17 May 1980 before working the 187 service back to Aberdare. Cynon-Dare was one of around half a dozen local identities introduced in 1980-82 following Market Analysis Projects (M.A.P.). RS4767 became RS1306 in January 1983 and was withdrawn and sold for scrap later that year.

*(Geoff Gould)*

MD1277 (SKG 891S) was a Leyland Redline 440EA minibus with high-backed seating for 20. The 440EA was a forward-control van chassis and was also specified by fellow NBC subsidiary Alder Valley. The Clubman 19 body was built by Ascough Ltd of Bessington, County Wicklow, Ireland. Western Welsh received four of these in 1977, numbered MD11-1477 (PKG 728R, SKG 891-3S) and allocated to Bridgend depot. They featured a sliding passenger door and were later down-seated to 19. From 22 August 1977 they began work on "Village Bus" services 291-296 based on the Cowbridge area, in this canary yellow and green livery. With cliffs and the Bristol Channel in the background, MD1277 climbs away from Southerndown beach on a gloomy 20 July 1980 and heads for Llantwit Major. Four similar buses numbered MD11-478 arrived in 1978, though MD11-1477 were replaced by larger vehicles in late 1981, and MD1277 (SKG 891S) had passed to Fernlea Pentecostal Church near Risca by August 1982.

*(John Jones)*

Love it or hate it, this view of UC278 (WUH 180T) shows off the NBC National white coach livery in all its corporate glory. It suited some vehicles better than others, but many would struggle to call it a livery. UC278 is a Plaxton Supreme III-bodied Leyland Leopard PSU3E/4R 49-seater, one of seven new to National Welsh in 1978 when, in addition, three 12-metre Leopards were added to the Jones of Aberbeeg fleet. The National Welsh examples were numbered UC1/2/6-1078 and were fitted with G2 gearboxes. UC278 is pictured at London's Victoria coach station in July 1980 having arrived on National Express service 660 from Swansea. This was described in publicity material as "The Red Dragon, a National Super coach service". UC278 became UC1163 in 1983 and UD163 by 1987.

*(Peter Keating)*

In 1972 Western Welsh received 34 Leyland Leopard PSU3B/4R models numbered 1521-54. These 36-foot buses had BET-style bodies built by Marshall of Cambridge. The first ten were 47-seat dual-purpose vehicles, but 1531-54 had bus type seating for 51, and featured luggage pens. They were distributed amongst six garages and were notable as the last traditional single-deckers delivered to Western Welsh prior to the introduction of what would become the NBC's standard bus, the Leyland National. In August 1974, 1531-54 were renumbered into the Red & White series as U1-2472 and we see U1272 (XBO 542K) departing Blackwood on 5 July 1980, working the service from Merthyr Tydfil to Newport. It was withdrawn from service around June 1982 after only ten years' service, and sold for scrap. It would seem that many of these Leopards had relatively short lives compared to National Welsh Bristol REs of around the same age.

*(John Jones)*

U4465 (FAX 296C) was a Leyland Tiger Cub with a Marshall body that had been new to Jones of Aberbeeg (124) in 1965. It originally had 45 dual-purpose type seats, which had been replaced with bus seats by April 1977. In April 1978 U4465 was hired by Jones to the newly-formed National Welsh, and was based at Abergavenny depot. This view on 6 September 1980 at Abergavenny shows a relatively smart-looking U4465, about to work a Brecon service and carrying Beaconsedge M.A.P. slip boards. It is thought that it was withdrawn from service later in the month before passing via a dealer to Scottish operator Wainhire of Stenhousemuir near Falkirk by March 1981. National Welsh hired six other vehicles from Jones during the period 1978 to 1980.

*(John Jones)*

As we have seen on page 14, Red & White was a keen Bristol MW user, though the fleet numbers of some of the MW service buses indicated the year they were built, but not necessarily when they entered service. As an example, U1-364 entered service in 1965 registered DAX 601-3C. The substantial 1965 MW intake comprised 27 45-seat buses numbered U1-2765 (DAX 604-30C) and entered service between February and October. U565 (DAX 608C) spent periods based at Tredegar, Monmouth and Ross-on-Wye depots, before passing to Western Welsh in January 1978 and becoming part of National Welsh in April that year. Here we see it in a very rural setting at Capel-y-Ffin near Llanthony on a glorious 6 September 1980. This is an area which had lost its bus services many years earlier and U565 was taking part in an enthusiasts' tour of former routes in the Abergavenny area. The excellent condition of the 15-year old bus was another reminder of Red & White days. It was one of the last remaining MWs in service when withdrawal came in 1982.

*(John Jones)*

Red & White's last Bristol MWs U1-1766 were completed in 1966, and the first fifteen entered service that year with registrations JAX 101-15D. U16/1766 were notable as they entered service at Aberdare in January 1967 as the only Bristol MW buses with E-suffix registrations (JAX 116/7E). On 8 September 1980, U1666 is seen crossing the River Usk approaching the historic Roman town of Caerleon. The bus has come from Newport and will later pass through picturesque Usk and Raglan before arriving at Monmouth, now its home depot. It was withdrawn in October 1980, but reinstated to the National Welsh "mothball" fleet in April 1981. In November 1981 it was earmarked for conversion to a towing vehicle but this never took place and JAX 116E was sold to a breaker in December 1984.

*(John Jones)*

Western Welsh received a substantial delivery of Leyland Nationals in 1975; of these there were just four shorter 10.3-metre examples. Numbered NS1-475 (KDW 323-6P) they seated 44 passengers and entered service in August. In October they became NS35-875, and by the end of the year all four had been hired to Red & White. NS3675 (KDW 324P) was based at Tredegar depot, and none of these buses were returned to Western Welsh until the latter part of 1977. There would be no further short Leyland Nationals until 1979. Now working for National Welsh and still based at Tredegar, NS3675 (KDW 324P) is seen on Steel Works Road, Ebbw Vale, on 8 September 1980. The bus appears to be working the 112 service to Bryn Y Gwynt which is part of a hillside housing estate high above, and to the west of Ebbw Vale. In 1983 it became NS1458 and then NS458 in 1986 and was later based at Crosskeys depot from where it was withdrawn during 1987, and is one of three similar buses acquired by Green, Kirkintilloch, in December that year.

*(John Jones)*

After placing the eighteen 36-foot Leyland Leopards into service in 1962 (page 6 upper), Western Welsh reverted to tried and trusted smaller Leyland Tiger Cubs to satisfy its requirement for single-deck buses for a further five years. The next Leopard buses entered service in May and June 1969 as 619-38 (PKG 619-38G) which, like the previous forty Tiger Cubs, had BET-style Marshall bodies. Fitted with 51 bus seats, they featured 4-speed semi-automatic gearboxes and single-speed rear axles. 629 became South Wales Transport 508 in March 1972, with the transfer of the Haverfordwest area services, while the remainder were renumbered U1-1969 in August 1974. In the National Welsh era they were to be found working from Barry, Bridgend, Crosskeys and Porth depots. U669 (PKG 624G) still looks to be in good order as it works out its final few weeks in service, bound for Cardiff on Lavernock Road, Lower Penarth on 2 September 1980. All nineteen survivors of this batch of Leopards had been taken out of service by the end of 1980.

*(Paul Dudley)*

Cwmbran-based U3566 (HBO 389D) is seen on Clarence Road as it leaves Pontypool on 4 October 1980 and, displaying an incorrectly set destination blind, is working a 130 via New Inn to Cwmbran. This service consisted of fourteen journeys from Pontypool to Cwmbran (Monday to Saturday), with five of them running through to Cardiff. U3566 had been new to Western Welsh as 1389 in September 1966, part of a batch of twenty Marshall-bodied Leyland Tiger Cubs received that year. Numbers 1385-94 were fitted with 43 bus seats, while 1375-84 had 41 coach-type seats. 1389 was renumbered U3566 by Western Welsh in the grand renumbering scheme of August 1974 and passed to National Welsh as such in 1978. It had been withdrawn and sold by December 1980.

*(John Jones)*

23

By the late 1970s large numbers of Leyland Nationals were in service throughout the UK and had become reasonably reliable vehicles. The fixed-head Leyland 510 engine was perceived to be its main weakness, so a revised National was developed which used the tried and tested Leyland 0.680 engine. The radiator was moved to the front of the bus which improved cooling, and the new vehicle was launched as the Leyland National 2 in November 1979. It proved to be a popular bus, and the National Bus Company took nearly 600 examples although only three came to National Welsh. They arrived in May 1980 as NS8011-3 (BUH 239-41V) and were 10.6-metre 44-seaters. NS8011/13 were initially allocated to Tredegar, while NS8012 went to Porth. NS8013 is only around six months old when photographed at Rhymney Bridge on 1 November 1980. It later became NS1493 and then NS493 in 1986. All three National 2s were sold prematurely, passing to Burnley and Pendle Transport in October 1988.

*(John Jones)*

The last vehicles delivered before Rhondda Transport was absorbed by Western Welsh in 1971 were three Leyland Leopard coaches with 49-seat Plaxton Panorama Elite bodies. New in July/August 1970, they were numbered 322-4 (YTX 322-4H) and were in the green and cream livery which had been adopted several years earlier for coaches and dual-purpose vehicles, and when similar Western Welsh vehicles became blue and cream. 322 and 323 were soon sold to Greenslades Tours of Exeter, while 324 initially became Western Welsh 2324.

By late 1971, 2324 had received Western Welsh coach livery and fleet number 109. In 1973 it was transferred to Jones of Aberbeeg as UC170J, while in August 1974 it became UC170, and UD170 in 1980. UD170 (YTX 324H) passed into National Welsh ownership on 1 January 1981 when the Jones fleet was absorbed. Freshly repainted into NBC dual-purpose livery, it basks in the sunshine at Cwmbran depot on 14 March 1981. In January 1983 it became UD1104 and had been withdrawn by the following December.

*(John Jones)*

25

HR5267 (JKG 483F) was one of the nine Daimler Fleetlines acquired from City of Cardiff Transport in 1979 and numbered HR50-867. A further six were acquired between January and March 1980 and took fleet numbers HR59-6467. Seven of them, including HR5267, were distributed between Monmouth, Ross and Cinderford garages from February 1980 while the remainder went to Bridgend, Barry and Penarth Road (Cardiff) later that year. Surprisingly, the first withdrawals took place as early as August 1981, while the last examples bowed out in December 1982. In this view at Pontypridd on 1 August 1981, HR5267 is caught on film as it leaves the bus station bound for Ferndale. The New Rhondda M.A.P. local identity branding is evident on what was the only Fleetline to be based at Porth depot.

*(John Jones)*

Western Welsh was very happy with its Tiger Cubs and it was only the impending end of production by Leyland which led to the first orders being placed for the 33-foot PSU4 Leopard. Delivered in 1971 as 1501-20, and featuring standard BET-style Willowbrook bodywork, the first ten were finished as 41-seat dual-purpose vehicles, and the remainder as 45-seat service buses. The latter were distributed between Barry, Bridgend and Penarth Road, Cardiff, depots. New in March 1971 as 1518, U871 (TKG 518J) is seen at Bridgend on 2 May 1981, leaving for Blackmill on a short working of the famous 172 Porthcawl – Aberdare service, formerly operated by Red & White. The local Welsh M.A.P. identity Glan-Ogwr refers to the River Ogmore/Ogwr which flows through Bridgend. Having spent its later National Welsh days modified to serve as a towing vehicle, TKG 518J is presently the subject of a major restoration project by the Cardiff Transport Preservation Group at Barry.

*(John Jones)*

To replace the eight Leyland Redline minibuses National Welsh purchased nine Bristol LHS6L midibuses with ECW bodywork. The first six arrived between December 1980 and February 1981 and were numbered MD8023-8 (GTX 758-63W) with 27 coach-type seats in their ECW bodies. At least four of this batch were soon repainted into Skyliner livery and based at Porth for services traversing some of the narrower streets in the Rhondda valleys. In this view we see MD8024 (GTX 759W) at Ferndale on 28 April 1981. It is bound for Porth travelling via Hendrefadog Street, Tylorstown, on Skyliner service 555. A further three similar buses were received in September 1981 as MD8114-6 (KWO 568-70X), and all nine were renumbered MD1391-9 in January 1983. After withdrawal GTX 759W passed to Guernseybus in December 1987 as 84 (19663). It returned to the mainland in May 1992 entering service with Curtis, Midsomer Norton, having reverted to GTX 759W.

*(Geoff Gould)*

27

During 1980, in an effort to replace older and non-standard types, National Welsh acquired twenty second-hand Leyland Nationals from other NBC fleets. Seventeen came from East Kent Road Car and comprised both 10.3-metre and 11.3-metre of these. New in as a 49-seater in October 1973 at a time when East Kent vehicles did not carry fleet numbers, it later became 1064. Upon entry into service as N7308-19, the 11.3-metre buses were initially distributed between Porth, Cwmbran, Crosskeys, Aberdare and Bridgend depots.

On 21 September 1981, and as the astronomical summer draws to a close, N7312 is seen deep in the Forest of Dean with the famous Speech House in the background. Built as a hunting lodge for Charles II, and now a hotel, it hosted the "Court of Speech" for Verderers and Free Miners of the Forest of Dean. The bus is heading south and will reach Lydney via the village of Parkend. N7312 became N1505 in 1983, and after deregulation was sold to the Provincial Bus Company.

*(John Jones)*

It is a cold and gloomy 19 December 1981 as UD6571 (VUH 185K) ascends Trebanog Hill with patches of snow evident all around. The coach is working hard as the trail of cars following now lie behind a smokescreen of partially-burnt diesel. UD6571 was new in August 1971, as one of six Plaxton Elite-bodied Leyland Leopards numbered 185-90. They were 49-seaters and the last pair, 188/9, did not enter service until March 1972. In the renumbering of 1974, they became UC1/271, UC1-372 and UC371 respectively, in what seems to be an unnecessary complication. In 1975, UC1-371 became UC65-771 while UC1-372 became UC49-5172. These coaches were downgraded to dual-purpose duties between June and October 1980 and received NBC dual-purpose livery having had their fleet number prefix changed from UC to UD. UD6571 was renumbered UD1113 in 1983 and was withdrawn from service by February/March 1984.

*(John Jones)*

From the same batch of vehicles as the subject on page 7, this much later views shows Bristol RELH RD5868 (OAX 2F) climbing Swansea Road, Merthyr Tydfil, on 20 February 1982. It is working the X6 to Cardiff via Aberdare, and carries very prominent Transglam M.A.P. branding. RD5868 was new in March 1968 as Red & White RC268 and was renumbered RC5868 in October 1975, and then RD5868 in October 1978 when it was demoted to a dual-purpose vehicle. In April 1980, its rather small coach-style destination blind apertures were replaced by those shown here which are far more appropriate for bus work. OAX 2F was withdrawn at the end of 1982, and on paper was allocated new fleet number RD1330. It did not return to service with its new fleet number, being sold for scrap in March 1983. Sister coach RC968 (OAX 9F) survives in active preservation in 2019 as a splendid reminder of these popular coaches.

(John Jones)

The Bristol VRT was never a popular vehicle in Scotland, so it was a surprise when Tayside Regional Council took delivery of a batch of 25 in 1977. They were long-wheelbase VRT/LL3 models with rather distinctive 83-seat Alexander dual-door bodies. The VRTs soon fell out of favour in a fleet that had by now adopted the Volvo Ailsa as its preferred double-decker, and many were sold in 1980/81. The Leyland-engined examples 206-10 (OSR 206-10R) passed to National Welsh in 1981 and were rebuilt to single door layout before entering service as HR61-577. HR6377 was based at Monmouth depot while the others were at Chepstow, and HR6177 (OSR 207R) is captured in a rural setting at Parkwall near Chepstow on 15 April 1982. These large useful buses were renumbered XR1951-5 in 1983 and all five received Red & White fleet names in October 1984. They later became XR861-5 and passed to Western Travel Ltd (Red & White) in February 1991 as 861-5.

*(John Jones)*

31

UD1874 (OWO 310M), a Leyland Leopard PSU3B/4R with a 53-seat Duple Dominant coach body, is parked outside Cardiff Castle on Monday 5 May 1982. It was one of a pair that were new in 1974 to Jones of Aberbeeg as UC6/774 (OWO 310/1M), and originally wore National white coach livery. They became UC18/974 in the 1975 renumbering, and received Jones' blue and white version of NBC dual-purpose livery in 1976/77. Both were later downgraded to dual-purpose status, and had received the appropriate NBC red and white livery by December 1980. UC18/974 passed to National Welsh on 1 January 1981 when the Jones fleet was fully absorbed. OWO 310M later became UD1134 from 1983 and UD134 in early 1986, and was withdrawn at the end of 1987. It later saw service with Berry of Crosshills near Keighley.

*(John Jones)*

N7319 (NFN 77M) was another of the former East Kent Road Car Leyland Nationals acquired by National Welsh in 1980 (see page 28). It was one of a batch of twenty similar vehicles (NFN 61-80M) delivered to East Kent in late 1973. Aberdare depot received N7319 in 1980 and it is seen making the turn from Penderyn Road onto Rhigos Road, Hirwaun, on service 186 to Pontypridd. The NFN batch was instantly recognisable as they had the larger roof pod whereas all the Series

One Nationals purchased new by National Welsh and its predecessors had the smaller pod. N7319 (NFN 77M) became N1512 in 1983 and then N512 in 1986 and was withdrawn in 1987 with the last examples of this particular batch of vehicles. Some were broken up by National Welsh at Bulwark, Chepstow, while others were sold on for further use.

*(John Jones)*

The 34 Leyland Leopards mentioned on page 19 entered service with Western Welsh between March and July 1972. The first ten were dual-purpose vehicles seating 47 and were numbered 1521-30 (XBO 521-30K). They were delivered in royal ivory and red livery, had blue upholstery and featured rear luggage lockers. UD2572 (XBO 521K) was new in March 1972 as 1521, and was initially based at Penarth Road depot in Cardiff. This batch became UD1-1072 in 1974 and then UD25-3472 in October 1975. UD2572 (XBO 521K) is about to cross Wood Street bridge over the River Taff in Cardiff in the late afternoon sunshine of 16 July 1982. It is thought the bus had been pressed into use on an Expresswest service, which explains why it has a very healthy load of passengers. UD2572 survived long enough to be renumbered UD1295 in early 1983 but had been withdrawn by the end of the year.

*(John Jones)*

Welcome purchases by National Welsh in 1980 were the eight Bristol RESL saloons from Bristol Omnibus Company. New in the summer of 1969, they had Leyland engines and 43-seat ECW bodies to the later style with deep flat windscreens and peaked roof domes. Numbered RS6960-7, they looked particularly smart in NBC poppy red livery as can be seen in this view of RS6963 (THU 348G) at Brecon on 12 September 1980. It is parked alongside the parish church of St Mary's before departing for Llanspyddid, a small village to the west of the town. Seven of these buses survived the renumbering of 1983 when THU 348G became RS1309 and was one of the last examples in service, being withdrawn and sold for scrap in the summer of 1984.

*(Geoff Gould)*

The only new vehicles for Western Welsh in 1970 were a batch of six 36-foot long Leyland Leopard coaches. They were numbered 179-84 (SKG 179-84H) and had Plaxton Panorama Elite bodies with seating for 49. They had five-speed gearboxes, two-speed rear axles and also featured power steering. 179 was transferred to Jones of Aberbeeg in April 1974 and was later renumbered UC270. The remaining vehicles became UC3-770 in August 1974. From March 1980 they were gradually downgraded to bus duties becoming UD3-770 and consequently gained NBC dual-purpose livery. Jones's UC270 was transferred back to National Welsh on 1 January 1981 where it became UD270 and received dual-purpose livery. In this view UD270 is a long way from home having been captured on film leaving Shrewsbury on 14 August 1982. It had been on an excursion to the famous Flower Show, an event which still takes place annually.

*(John Jones)*

Ynysybwl is a large village and former mining community in the Cwm Clydach valley and about four miles from Pontypridd. The bus in this shot is former Red & White Bristol RESL6L RS4271 (YAX 594J) with a 47-seat ECW, body one of a batch of ten similar vehicles new in 1971/72 as RS1-1071. They became RS42-5171 in October 1975 and all passed to National Welsh in April 1978. Aberdare based RS4271 is seen in Augustus Street, Ynysybwl, on 22 October 1982 on service 183 from Pontypridd to Old Ynysybwl. In the background is Lady Windsor Colliery, and beyond on the hillside is its waste coal tip. The colliery closed in 1988 after 104 years of high-quality coal production. The bus was renumbered RS1314 in January 1983 and was withdrawn from service by November 1984 and scrapped.

*(John Jones)*

By 1972 West Midlands PTE was experiencing difficulties obtaining sufficient numbers of new Daimler Fleetlines so it turned to the Bristol VRT and ordered 200 with 76-seat MCW bodywork for delivery between 1972 and 1976. It became the largest fleet of Bristol VRTs with a single operator, though many of them were sold after a relatively short life. National Welsh took nineteen examples in 1982 plus an additional pair for spare parts. The serviceable buses were allocated fleet numbers HR7434-52 and in January 1983 they were renumbered XR1956-74. On 20 November 1982 we are back in Pontypridd and are presented with this fine study of HR7438 (TOE 430N) on a run to Maerdy, though little care seems to have been taken setting the blind. HR7438 had only recently entered service with National Welsh and became XR1960 in January 1983.

*(John Jones)*

Your author has a soft spot for the Bristol RE and could not resist another shot of one of the former Red & White RESLs in action. This is RS4471 (YAX 596J) and it is getting the opportunity of a good long run as it passes through Machen on a sunny Saturday 27 November 1982. It is working the 149 from Rhymney Bridge to Newport via Bargoed and Caerphilly, a service shared with Rhymney Valley District Council.

The bus was new as Red & White RS371 in May 1971 when it was allocated to Chepstow depot. At the time of this photograph over 11 years later, it was presumably working from a Gwent depot, probably Tredegar, though officially allocated to Aberdare. Sadly, it was sold for scrap in 1983.

*(John Jones)*

This image taken in Bridgend on 26 March 1983 makes for an interesting comparison with the one on page 27 taken almost two years earlier. Here we have UD1283 (TKG 501J), which was another of the twenty Leyland Leopard PSU4 saloons delivered in 1971. However this particular bus was one of the ten fitted with 41 high-backed seats in its Willowbrook bodywork. As a reminder of this, the bus carries NBC dual-purpose livery and still has its full complement of aluminium trim.

It was originally Western Welsh 1501, entering service in March 1971 at Cwmbran depot, and 1501-10 were the last vehicles delivered in Western Welsh's blue and royal ivory dual-purpose livery. It was subject to much renumbering in its time, and eventually became UD1283 in January 1983 when the "year of build" numbers were dispensed with. Numbers 1270-99 were reserved for Leyland saloons and semi-coaches.

*(John Jones)*

Half a dozen of the 21 Bristol RESLs new to Red & White in 1967 survived into 1983, and were renumbered RS1301-6 in the new series. RS1301 (LAX 101E), numerically the first example, was also the last survivor. As RS2967 it moved from Aberdare to Tredegar in June 1976 and on to Brynmawr in September 1980 by which time it was in National Welsh ownership. It was back at Tredegar by April 1981, which is where we see it on 10 April 1983. RS1301 was officially withdrawn in the following September but never actually came out of service. By December 1983 it was back at Aberdare, and still with its Gwent Vales M.A.P. vinyls. The final transfer for this bus was across to Chepstow in February 1984. Here it gained Wye-Dean local branding, but was withdrawn the following May. RS1301 was purchased for preservation, and eventually restored to original condition by the Re-liance Bus Group in 1997.

(Andrew Wiltshire)

In 1981/82 National Welsh received a dozen Leyland Leopard PSU3F/4R models fitted with Willowbrook 003 coach bodies. They were the subject of a somewhat protracted delivery process with UC8108-13 (KWO562-7X), 46-seaters that arrived between September and November 1981 followed by UC8201-6 (KWO 556-61X) which were taken into stock between March and May 1982 and were 47-seaters. Things were however simplified a little with the 1983 renumbering as they became UC1181-92 respectively, but the registrations were still in two out of sequence blocks. UC1189 (KWO 558X), a 47-seater, is seen leaving Port Talbot bus station in April 1983. It is allocated to Expresswest duties which will see it working anywhere between Pembrokeshire and Bristol. This batch of coaches had been downgraded to dual-purpose duties by 1987 and numbered UD181-92. Finally, to free-up fleet numbers for new Bustler minibuses, they became UD381-92 in March 1988.

(Cliff Essex)

Over 1000 Leyland Olympians were supplied to NBC subsidiaries but National Welsh received just ten examples in the spring of 1982. They had Gardner 6LXB engines, standard 77-seat ECW bodies and were numbered HR8207-16 (MUH 281-90X). Five were allocated to Barry while the remainder were based at Porth, and in January 1983 they became HR1851-60. Having just left the bus station, HR1852 (MUH 282X) is seen passing the construction site of the new police station at Pontypridd on 22 October 1983. The bus is heading from Cardiff to Maerdy on service 332, and is wearing an overall advertisement livery for CBC Radio 221. CBC (Cardiff Broadcasting Company) was an early independent radio station launched in Cardiff in April 1980 and later became known as Red Dragon Radio. HR1852 was renumbered HR852 in 1986 but was destroyed by fire at Barry depot on 23 August of that year. Its remains were scrapped in February 1987.

*(John Jones)*

In April/May 1972 Red & White received 13 Bristol RELH dual-purpose saloons numbered RD1-1372. They featured a return to Gardner engines for the first time since 1966, 47 coach-style seats and were finished in an attractive cream and red livery. A fourteenth similar vehicle went to Jones of Aberbeeg as RD1472J. In their early days they were engaged on limited stop and express services and often turned up at London's Victoria coach station. The Red & White vehicles were distributed between Tredegar, Brynmawr, Chepstow, Newport and Aberdare depots. In October 1975 they were renumbered RD35-4772, and all passed to National Welsh in 1978. On 17 December 1983, CWO 290K was still classed as a dual-purpose vehicle and in standard NBC dual-purpose livery. It had then been renumbered RD1369, and was engaged on more mundane duties, returning from Pentwyn to Pontypool when seen near the rugby club in Pentrepiod. RD1369 was one of the last survivors of this batch when it was taken out of service by September 1984.

*(John Jones)*

We are now in the Chepstow area on 5 May 1984 for this view of R1354 (YWO 692K) at Beachley Church. The bus is working the well-known service 12 from Bulwark via Chepstow town centre, and will terminate near the army barracks at Beachley over the border in Gloucestershire. Beachley is on a narrow peninsula of land at the point where the River Wye flows into the Severn Estuary. It lies in the shadow of the original Severn and Wye bridges that opened in September 1966. New as Red & White R771 in September 1971, it was one of nine Bristol RELL6Ls delivered that year (R1-4, 7-1171) with 53-seat ECW bodywork. R7-1171 was a diverted Western Welsh order, and Jones of Aberbeeg received two similar vehicles (R5/671J). R771 was renumbered R3771 in 1975 and after transfer to National Welsh became R1354 in 1983. It was withdrawn from Chepstow depot within a few weeks of this photograph being taken.

*(John Jones)*

Leaving the grounds of Butlins Holiday Park at Barry Island on 7 May 1984 is Leopard UC1131 (RBO 193M). This famous venue, one of two in Wales, opened in 1966 and was operated by Butlins until 1986 after which it had a number of owners. It closed in 1996 and was demolished to make way for new housing. Five Duple Dominant-bodied Leopards were delivered in 1974; RBO 191-3M were 49-seat PSU3B/4RT models, while RBO 194/5M were the shorter PSU4B/4RT variety with 41-seats. They were allocated Western Welsh fleet numbers 191-5, but entered service as UC1-574 in the numbering scheme introduced that year. In 1975 they were renumbered UC13-774 and a few of them spent periods on hire to Red & White during 1976/77. In July 1981 UC1474 was badly damaged by fire while on a London service and was scrapped. The survivors were then renumbered UC1130-3 in 1983 and later downgraded to dual-purpose status. They were withdrawn as UD130-3 between November 1986 and November 1987.

*(John Jones)*

In May 1971 Red & White received a pair of 51-seat Plaxton Elite-bodied Bristol RELH6L coaches numbered RC1/271. Jones of Aberbeeg received a similar pair the following month numbered RC3/471J, followed by RC173 (NWO 102M), though in National white, in 1973. Four similar coaches were delivered to Red & White in the summer of 1973 as RC2-573 (NAX 3-6M), which were 47-seaters in National white livery and were split equally between Chepstow and Cardiff (Gelligaer Street) depots. RC2-573 were downgraded from coach (RC) to dual-purpose status (RD) between December 1982 and July 1983, and renumbered RC1125, RD1126 or RC1127/8 in January 1983. On 12 May 1984, NAX 5M, now RD1127 is seen climbing Fair View, Cefn Fforest between Bargoed and Blackwood on the Saturday X86 service to Bristol. All four RELHs were transferred to Porth in 1985 and RD1127 was the last of this quartet in service. It was renumbered RD127 in 1986 and withdrawn at the end of that year and sold for scrap.

*(John Jones)*

The initial 12-metre coaches for National Welsh arrived in the first half of 1980 numbered UC8014-22 (BUH 220-8V). They were Leyland Leopard PSU5D/4R chassis with Plaxton Supreme IV bodies seating 57 though this was reduced to 53 before they entered service. In January 1983 they became UC1172-80, and UC1174 (BUH 222V) is seen here in National Holidays livery at the Gelligaer Street depot, Cardiff. At Barry depot on 23 August 1986, a fire broke out in the engine compartment of UC1174, which, by then, was registered AAL 404A. The fire also badly damaged similar coach 1178 (AAL 303A), and completely destroyed Leyland Olympian HR852 (see page 41). Both coach chassis were renovated and given new Plaxton Paramount III 3200 bodies in 1987. The remaining seven coaches in the batch were given similar Plaxton bodies in 1988.

*(Peter Keating)*

The last two Bristol RELHs with ECW bus body shells for the Western Welsh group of companies were delivered to Jones of Aberbeeg. They were Gardner-powered RD673 (HAX 305L) which entered service in April 1973, and Leyland-powered RD174 (OWO 309M) which followed in July 1974 both in Jones's blue version of NBC dual-purpose livery. The latter was renumbered RD2674 in October 1975, and both passed to National Welsh on 1 January 1981. They received poppy red and white and in 1983 they were renumbered RD1377 and RD1142 respectively. On 26 May 1984 RD1142 (OWO 309M) is seen in Griffithstown having passed under the railway bridge in New Road at the junction with Station Road. It is working service X30, which was introduced on 6 December 1982 and linked Pontypool via Cwmbran with Cardiff. This bridge once carried the Eastern Valley line which ran up through Pontypool Crane Street Station to Blaenavon though both the railway bridge and embankment have since been removed and the road widened.

*(John Jones)*

The last four Bristol RESL saloons were delivered to Red & White Services in March 1972 as RS7-1071 (CAX 307-10K) following on from RS1-671 which actually had been received in 1971 (see pages 36 and 38). RS971 (CAX 309K), a 47-seater, was based when new at Lydney depot and in the 1975 renumbering became RS5071. By the time it passed to National Welsh in 1978 it was working from Monmouth depot along with RS5171 (CAX 310K), and in 1983 this batch of four buses became RS1320-3. This splendid view of RS1322 (CAX 309K) was taken at Poplar Road, Georgetown, Tredegar, on 12 May 1984, as the bus makes its way a little further down the Sirhowy valley to the Peacehaven estate. RS1320-3 were all withdrawn in 1984 and sold for scrap.

*(John Jones)*

47

The Leyland Tiger was launched in 1981 and was a replacement for the Leopard which had been in production in various forms since 1959. The Tiger was a mid-engined chassis aimed primarily at the coaching market and National Welsh had ordered two with Duple Goldliner coach bodies for Rapide work. However they arrived in July 1983 with Duple Caribbean bodies. Like the Goldliner, the Caribbean body was aimed at the higher end of the market and initially was only available as a 12-metre vehicle. These two coaches were numbered XC1251/2 (SDW 910/1Y), had seating for 46 plus a hostess, and were fitted with a toilet. On a glorious Sunday morning, XC1251 is seen leaving Nantddu Terrace in Edwardsville and will reach Pontypridd around ten minutes later. It is 20 May 1984, and the first day of operation of the 508 Aberdare-Merthyr-Pontypridd-Caerphilly-London, National Express Rapide service. This road was still the A470 at this time as the replacement dual carriageway had then only reached as far north as Abercynon. XC1251/2 were later renumbered XC251/2 in February 1986, and were re-registered TWO 76 and 20 AAX a month later, using marks from old Red & White vehicles.

*(John Jones)*

The last Bristols for Red & White were six RELH6L coaches that entered service between April and June 1974. For the first time they featured ECW's Mark 2 coach body which was introduced in 1972 and available as a pure coach or to bus grant specification. It featured a standard Plaxton windscreen and, as is obvious in this image, the side glazing was flat to save costs. These 47-seat coaches were numbered RC1-674 (OWO 303-8M) and became RC20-574 in 1975. They passed to National Welsh in 1978 and in 1982/83 were downgraded to dual-purpose status, before becoming RD1136-41 in the new series. On 21 July 1984, RD1137 (OWO 304M) is seen on Sycamore Road South, Sebastopol, while circumnavigating the Kemys Fawr housing estate. It is working the X30 from Pontypool to Cardiff, and is wearing the local coach livery from this period. The first example was withdrawn in early 1985, and RD1137 bowed out in February 1986.

*(John Jones)*

Branded for the Pontypool-Cwmbran-Cardiff X30 service, UC1154 (PKG 725R) is seen in Victoria Street, Old Cwmbran, on 28 January 1985. This coach was one of three Leyland Leopard PSU3E/4RT models with 49-seat Duple Dominant I Express bodies delivered to Jones of Aberbeeg in April/May 1977. They passed to National Welsh with the Jones fleet on 1 January 1981, and became UC1152-4 exactly two years later. In this view UC1154 is wearing the local coach livery that was introduced in the early 1980s and was sometimes referred to as the "venetian blind" livery. PKG 725R was one of fifteen National Welsh Leyland Leopards that passed to OK Travel in 1989.

*(John Jones)*

Of the twenty second-hand Leyland Nationals acquired by National Welsh in 1980, eight were of the shorter 41-seat, 10.3-metre variety. Two of them had originated with Maidstone and District while the remainder had come from East Kent Road Car. SJG 336N had previously been East Kent 1336, new in 1974, and became National Welsh NS7431 in September 1980 entering service from Aberdare depot. In this view taken on 23 February 1985, the bus has now become NS1452 and has received Cynon-Dare local branding, reflecting its home depot. It is seen at Bryntirion, Matthewstown, which is situated between Penrhiwceiber and Abercynon. The bus is bound for the Penlocks area of Abercynon, through which the Glamorganshire Canal passed many decades earlier. NS1452 (SJG 336N) was still owned in 1987 but had left the fleet by 1989.  .

*(John Jones)*

The Western Welsh group of companies did not receive their first Leyland National until the autumn of 1974. This was well over a year after neighbouring NBC fleet South Wales Transport introduced the type. The first batch comprised five 52-seat 11.3-metre models for Western Welsh numbered N1-574 (GHB 787-91N), and featured the newly-introduced smaller roof pod. One of them was based at Penarth Road, Cardiff, depot and four at Crosskeys while Red & White had also received five similar vehicles by the end of the year. N574 was hired to Red & White at Aberdare from August to December 1975, and for part of this time carried Red & White fleet names. N1-574 passed to National Welsh in April 1978 and were renumbered N1513-7 on 1 January 1983. This superb view depicts N1517 (GHB 791N) leaving Cefnpennar on 8 March 1985 bound for Perthcelyn, a housing estate high up on the opposite side of the Cynon Valley which it will reach via Mountain Ash town centre.

*(Geoff Gould)*

The second batch of Leyland Nationals delivered to the Western Welsh group of companies between December 1974 and May 1975 comprised twenty 11.3-metre models. Western Welsh received N7-1175 while Red & White took N6-1074 and N1-6/12-475, all 52-seaters. Just to make things more confusing, Jones of Aberbeeg received N11/274 as 49-seaters. Former Red & White N674 (GHB 677N) has just descended Castleford Hill and is crossing the River Wye into Chepstow, and Wales, on 8 March 1985. The bus is using the original cast iron Old Wye Bridge designed by John Rastrick and dating from 1816. Despite the destination shown, N674 is actually returning from Beachley. It became N1518 in 1983 and N518 in 1986 and, after sale, it was rebuilt into a Leyland National Greenway by June 1994, becoming Midland Fox (3250) and re-registered GIL 2156.

*(Geoff Gould)*

The last Leyland Leopards delivered new to National Welsh were a trio of 12-metre PSU5E/4R models with unusual ECW B51 53-seat coach bodies. The booked registrations MUH 291-3X were cancelled and they entered service in December 1982 as PKG 104-6Y. They were almost immediately renumbered from UC8217-9 to UC1193-5 and started work on limited stop Expresswest services between West Wales and Bristol. UC1193 (PKG 104Y) is seen about to enter Cardiff bus station on 20 July 1985 on its way to Bristol. In 1986 this trio became UC193-5, were re-registered AAL 528/62/3A in 1987, and renumbered UC893-5 in March 1988. To confuse matters further, by 1992 they had become simply 893-5, with 893/4 now registered UDW 640/39Y respectively. After sale by National Welsh, PKG 104Y, now masquerading as UDW 640Y, went on to work in Scotland for Bellview Coaches (John Walker) of Paisley.

*(John Jones)*

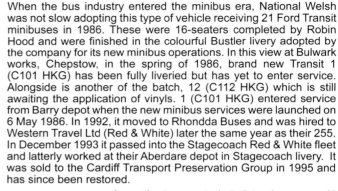

When the bus industry entered the minibus era, National Welsh was not slow adopting this type of vehicle receiving 21 Ford Transit minibuses in 1986. These were 16-seaters completed by Robin Hood and were finished in the colourful Bustler livery adopted by the company for its new minibus operations. In this view at Bulwark works, Chepstow, in the spring of 1986, brand new Transit 1 (C101 HKG) has been fully liveried but has yet to enter service. Alongside is another of the batch, 12 (C112 HKG) which is still awaiting the application of vinyls. 1 (C101 HKG) entered service from Barry depot when the new minibus services were launched on 6 May 1986. In 1992, it moved to Rhondda Buses and was hired to Western Travel Ltd (Red & White) later the same year as their 255. In December 1993 it passed into the Stagecoach Red & White fleet and latterly worked at their Aberdare depot in Stagecoach livery. It was sold to the Cardiff Transport Preservation Group in 1995 and has since been restored.

*(www.the-transport-photo-interchange.co.uk)*

Ordered by Western Welsh, HR808 (VHB 672S) was delivered to National Welsh as HR3378 in June 1978. It was one of a batch of nine similar ECW-bodied Bristol VRTs, four of which had been ordered for Red & White. HR3378 was renumbered HR1808 in 1983 and HR808 in 1986 as seen here on 22 May that year. The bus is in Aberrhondda Road, Porth, opposite the entrance to the bus garage, and is bound for Maerdy at the head of the Rhondda Fach valley. It is in overall NBC poppy red prior to the application of an advertising livery for Youngers Bitter, which it had received by 19 July. After the demise of National Welsh, VHB 672S passed to JBS Coaches of Bedford in 1992 and to Stephenson of Rochford, Essex, by September 1996. Around 1999/2000 it was converted into a caravan for a tour of Europe and Africa. By 2005, and now in Danish ownership, VHB 672S had received a Gardner engine but was completely destroyed by fire in November 2008, after an incident involving camping gas.

*(John Jones)*

National Welsh took its first Leyland Tigers in the spring and early summer of 1983 when twenty with Plaxton Paramount 3200 bodies numbered UC1196-1215 (SDW 912-31Y) arrived. UC1196-202 were conventional 51-seater coaches, while others had an on-board toilet. In 1986 the batch was renumbered UC196-215 as illustrated by UC198 (SDW 914Y) at Carmarthen on 28 May 1986. It is working Traws Cambria service 701 from Aberystwyth to Cardiff in a special livery promoting Bilidowcar, a Welsh language children's TV programme created in 1975. Originally broadcast on BBC Wales, in 1982 it transferred to the newly-created S4C channel. By 1987 many of this batch had received new dateless registrations to disguise their age, and UC198 duly became AAX 450A. By 1990 it had been renumbered UD898 and wore post-privatisation Swiftlink livery. The following year, it passed to Western Travel Ltd (Red & White), and in December 1993 was absorbed into the Stagecoach Red & White fleet as 898.

*(John Jones)*

Duple launched its Laser body at the 1982 Commercial Motor Show as a replacement for the Dominant range. The Laser was intended to compete with the influx of continental coaches from the likes of Bova, Neoplan, Van Hool and Jonckheere. It was a normal-height coach body, Duple's high-floor model being the Caribbean. In 1983/84 National Welsh received nineteen Duple Laser-bodied Leyland Tigers numbered UC1216-34 (A216-34 VWO). Most were 49-seaters, but UC1229-34 seated just 47, and were fitted with a toilet. A223 VWO, which was new in April 1984 and renumbered UC223 in 1986, is seen at Bournemouth on 23 July 1986 whilst engaged on a tour and wearing the revised (and somewhat improved) National Express coach livery. By 1989 it had become UC923 and had been re-registered AKG 162A. After the demise of National Welsh, this coach could be found operating with Stagecoach Bluebird in 1994.

*(the late John Wiltshire)*

The last Bristol VRTs delivered to National Welsh were a batch of twenty numbered LR8041-60 (GTX 738-57W). They had 74-seat ECW bodywork to a height of just 13ft 5in, and entered service between August and December 1980. On a glorious 26 July 1986 we see an immaculate LR722 (GTX 746W), originally LR8049, entering Ebbw Vale and passing Libanus Congregational Church. LR722 carries Gwent Vales M.A.P. branding and is working the former Jones of Aberbeeg service from Newport which had recently been extended to Tredegar. Thirteen buses from this batch including LR722 passed to Western Travel Ltd (Red & White) in February 1991 and subsequently to Stagecoach in 1992. It then transferred to Stagecoach Midland Red South in 1993 as their 941. In 1999 GTX 746W embarked on a new sightseeing career in the USA with New York Apple Tours. This proved short-lived and it was scrapped by 2001.

*(John Jones)*

Leyland National ND407 (KDW 353P) passes St John's Church, Libanus Road, Ebbw Vale, also on 26 July 1986. The church has recently been converted into a residential dwelling while the older building on the right of the picture was demolished some time ago. ND407 was one of the first batch of dual-purpose-seated Leyland Nationals for the Western Welsh group of companies. Seventeen vehicles were delivered in the latter part of 1975 as ND39-5575 (KDW 347-63P) of which ND41-675 were allocated to Red & White. They passed to National Welsh in 1978, and became ND1403-8 on 1 January 1983. Having had its fleet number reduced by 1000 to ND407 earlier in the year, this well turned out Leyland National is working the X4 to Cardiff via Merthyr Tydfil and Pontypridd.

*(John Jones)*

In the late summer of 1976 Western Welsh placed in service four 49-seat Duple Dominant-bodied Leyland Leopard PSU3C/4R models. They were numbered UC1-476 (NWO 446-9R) and worked National Express duties including the London service, and were soon equipped for one-person operation. Red & White received UC5/676 in early 1977 which were similar in most respects. By 1981 UC1-476 had become UD1-476 eventually gaining dual-purpose livery and becoming UD1146-9 in 1983 and UD146-9 in 1986. UD148 (NWO 448R) is seen here in the short-lived Quicklink livery arriving at Merthyr Tydfil from Cardiff on 19 August 1986. Service X4 will take it on to Tredegar, Ebbw Vale, Brynmawr and Abergavenny. NWO 448R was amongst fifteen Duple-bodied Leyland Leopards purchased by OK Travel of Bishop Auckland in 1989, when it was claimed that many were found to be in poor condition and required extensive rebuilding.

*(John Jones)*

The events that followed Deregulation Day on 26 October 1986 would drastically change the bus industry as we knew it. Further new additions to the Bustler minibus fleet, and hot on the heels of the Ford Transits was a batch of 29 Iveco 49/10 minibuses based on the light commercial van chassis. These had 21-seat bodies by Robin Hood Vehicle Builders of Locks Heath near Southampton. Arriving in September 1986, the Ivecos were numbered 22-50 (D22-50 KAX) and were initially allocated to Aberdare, Cwmbran and Porth depots. One of the latter, pictured at Tonypandy on 2 July 1987, was 32 (D32 KAX). Porth later gained all the Cwmbran-based Ivecos which had been replaced by new Sherpas. 32 survived until the end of National Welsh in February 1992.

*(the late John Wiltshire)*

National Welsh re-introduced the Red & White fleet name for vehicles operating in the east Monmouthshire and Gloucestershire garages in October 1984. This is exemplified by dual-purpose Leyland National ND413 (KDW 359P) which has just arrived in Cardiff on the lengthy X73 service from Gloucester on 9 May 1987. ND413 entered service with Western Welsh in November 1975 as ND5175, though it was originally to have been numbered ND1375. By 1978, when National Welsh was created, ND5175 was one of three Leyland Nationals allocated to Ross depot. In an attempt to cover some of the losses that had been incurred, on 1 February 1991 National Welsh sold its "Red & White" area of the business to Western Travel Ltd, Cheltenham, the parent company of Cheltenham and Gloucester Omnibus Co. ND413 (KDW 359P) subsequently passed into this new Red & White operation.

*(the late John Wiltshire)*

National Welsh received a further three ECW-bodied Bristol LHS midibuses in September 1981 and these entered service as MD8114-6 (KWO 568-70X). They were delivered in the green and canary yellow "Village Bus" livery for use on the special services in the Cowbridge area. They were renumbered MD1397-9 in January 1983 and MD397-9 in February 1986. Upon the loss of the Village Bus services to Bebb Travel in 1986/87, MD397/8 were transferred to Brynmawr depot and, along with MD391/2, were repainted into Hilltoppa livery in October 1986 for use on special services in the Hilltop area of Ebbw Vale. MD397 (KWO 568X) is seen appropriately descending a hill in Ebbw Vale on 12 May 1987. Hilltoppa was a short-lived entity and all four buses were withdrawn in December that year and sold to Guernseybus.

*(Geoff Gould)*

Having been sold to its management in May 1987, National Welsh struggled to make any profit in an environment of fierce competition. Since 1984, vehicles running out of National Welsh depots at Cwmbran, Chepstow, Brynmawr and Ross were carrying Red & White fleet names in place of National Welsh and Cymru Cenedlaethol. There were still six former West Midlands PTE Bristol VRTs left in National Welsh service in 1987 and, with their MCW bodywork, they added some variety to the fleet. One of the survivors is XR972 (NOB 405M) which is seen running into Newport bus station from Chepstow on 10 September 1987. Its destination blind is quite badly set though the bus is looking very smart and free from advertisements. XR972 and the other survivors were withdrawn by early 1989.

*(the late John Wiltshire)*

Another of the low-height VRTs is included as this one has a rather attractive overall advertising livery. LR721 (GTX 745W) was new as LR8048 in September 1980 but was renumbered LR721 in 1983. In this view taken on 7 May 1988, LR721 has left the bus station at Newport, and is making its way out of town on a 56 working to Tredegar via Ynysddu and Blackwood. It is seen at the top of Queensway about to cross the bridge over the South Wales main railway line, and Newport station can clearly be seen in the background. Your author is not familiar with Hunter Bitter, but has a feeling he has not missed anything special in this respect. As for the VRT, LR721 (GTX 745W) was still working for National Welsh in 1991, but was later scrapped.

*(the late John Wiltshire)*

The Bustler minibus network played a significant role in National Welsh operations between 1986 and 1992. Whilst not providing great levels of comfort, these little buses often offered the travelling public five to ten minute frequencies. As a result of this, levels of patronage rose in towns such as Aberdare, Cwmbran, Porth and Tredegar. In its very distinctive livery, Bustler 84 (E84 OUH) is seen in the upper Cynon Valley at Gwladys Street on the housing estate at Penywaun whilst working from Hirwaun via Aberdare to Pontypridd on 13 May 1988. Number 84 is a Freight Rover Sherpa 405 with 20-seat bodywork completed by Carlyle to their Citybus 2 design and entered service in August 1987.

*(Geoff Gould)*

Minibuses were seen as a solution to a number of problems in the latter half of the 1980s, and they were also relatively cheap to lease or purchase. As noted above, they often gave the public high frequency services and, in some cases their success meant that bigger buses were required to replace them on some routes. Bustler operation in the Caerphilly and Rhymney Valley areas increased following the departure of Inter Valley Link from the bus scene in 1989. In this view taken at Caerphilly bus station on 20 March 1989, there is no getting away from the fact that the Carlyle-bodied Sherpa minibus has little more to offer than earlier van conversions. 174 (E174 TWO) is engaged on one of the Caerphilly area services as it enters the bus station on route C12, from Senghenydd.

*(Geoff Gould)*

Formerly Rhymney Valley DC until October 1986, Inter Valley Link Ltd (IVL) did not purchase any new vehicles until the autumn of 1988. At this point they placed in service seventeen short-wheelbase MCW Metroriders numbered 101-117. Their smart light grey livery, enhanced by red and green stripes and carried "Inter Valley Classic" branding. These would be the only new vehicles delivered to Inter Valley Link which sold out to National Welsh on 21 March 1989 and ceased to operate on 1 April. The Metroriders passed to National Welsh, as 2101-17, and all were transferred to Merthyr from 5 June 1989. Still in its IVL grey livery, 2111 (F111 YWO) is photographed in the bus station at Merthyr Tydfil two days later.

*(the late John Wiltshire)*

The six Leyland Tiger coaches that were delivered to National Welsh in 1986 were significant as they were the last new Leylands for this operator. They were numbered XC259-64 and were delivered in National Express Rapide livery apart from XC264 which was finished for National Holidays. They were TRCTL11/3RH models which featured a semi-automatic hydracyclic gearbox and 48-seat Plaxton Paramount 3500 II bodywork complete with a toilet. By 1988 they were renumbered XC959-64 and most were eventually down-seated to 46. On 29 January 1989 we see XC963 (C263 GUH) arriving at Cardiff airport and it is now wearing National Holidays livery. This coach was new in March 1986 and was originally based at Cwmbran depot. When National Welsh went out of business, four of these coaches were exported to Ireland in 1992, and C263 GUH followed them in 1994 becoming 86-G-816 with Donoghue of Clarinbridge. XC962 (C262 GUH) remained on the UK mainland and is now preserved.

*(the late John Wiltshire)*

In 1988 six Freight Rover Sherpas were delivered in a blue livery and branded as "Taff-Ely Bustler". The vehicles were 215-9 and 226, all of which were completed by Carlyle as 20-seaters. Under the terms of the takeover of Taff-Ely Transport, these minibuses would be used on former Taff-Ely services in the Pontypridd area in their blue livery for a period of two years, and were initially based at Aberdare until a new base in Pontypridd was opened in March 1990. On 27 July 1989 we have 218 (F218 AKG), 226 (F226 AWO) and one other, lined up at the Tesco superstore, Upper Boat. The base at Pontypridd closed in October 1990 and its allocation was distributed amongst Bedwas, Aberdare and Merthyr Tydfil depots. Most, if not all, of the Taff-Ely Bustlers had their fleet names removed by March 1991.

*(the late John Wiltshire)*

During June and July 1986 National Welsh transformed two of its Bristol VRTs into convertible open-top buses. The vehicles chosen were HR817/8 (VHB 677/8S) which were from the nine ECW-bodied VRTs delivered to National Welsh in June and July of 1978. They had been new as HR42/378, becoming HR1817/8 in 1983 and HR817/8 in early 1986. In their new role they became HO817/8 and began work from 20 July 1986 on a new service X99 which ran from Cardiff to Barry Island via Ely and Gibbonsdown. HO817 is seen in Cardiff bus station on 22 July 1989 wearing an overall advert livery promoting locally produced Thayers ice cream. In 1990 these buses were exchanged with Crosville Wales for a pair of slightly newer Gardner-powered Bristol VRTs. After a number of subsequent owners, both ended up with Prestige Tours, Glasgow, in 2002. VHB 677S was destroyed by fire the same year, but VHB 678S has since had a somewhat chequered career in preservation.

*(the late John Wiltshire)*

National Welsh took over the operations of Taff-Ely Transport on 5 September 1988, and with this came a number of vehicles, only some of which dovetailed into the NWOS fleet. Taff-Ely purchased three East Lancs-bodied Dennis Lancet saloons in 1984 and numbered them 35-7 (A35-7 XBO). These passed to National Welsh as NS495-7 in November 1988, but were renumbered DS495-7 in January 1989 when it was realised these were not Leyland Nationals. They were initially based at Aberdare but later moved to Bedwas. DS497 is seen entering Merthyr bus station on 18 August 1989. It is in the attractive livery that was first introduced in December 1987. Lacking a destination blind it is presumably working the X4 to Cardiff. Despite their relative youth, these buses were not popular, and were destined to have a brief career with National Welsh. They were withdrawn by February 1991, and after a period in store they passed to Rhondda Buses Ltd in May 1992. They had moved on to Vanguard Coaches of Bedworth near Coventry by November, where they received a smart blue and white livery. All three passed to Midland Red South in 1995.

*(John Jones)*

On 5 September 1988, and after a period of financial difficulty, Taff-Ely Transport Ltd was sold to National Welsh. The deal included sixteen buses, but not the garage which remained with the Borough Council. At the end of operations the Taff-Ely fleet strength was only around twenty vehicles, and amongst them was a pair of East Lancs-bodied Dodge S56 midibuses dating from 1987. They featured 24 high-backed seats in their rather ungainly bodies, and were similar to eight vehicles delivered to Newport Transport. National Welsh numbered them 344/5

(D38/9 NDW) and by August 1989 they were based at Bridgend depot and branded as a Vale Bustler. In this view we are in the Vale of Glamorgan at Broughton near Wick on 8 August 1989. 345 is turning out of Chapel Road onto Water Street and will continue its trundle around the lanes before reaching Llantwit Major. Fortunately, the Dodge appears to have picked up a passenger or two along the way.

*(Geoff Gould)*

On 21 March 1989 the services and vehicles of Inter Valley Link Ltd were acquired by National Welsh Omnibus Services Ltd. The deal did not include the garages, and from midnight on 1 April, the operations together with thirty vehicles passed to National Welsh. The last vehicles acquired by Inter Valley Link were four Leyland Leopard PSU3E/4R models with 49-seat Duple Dominant II bodywork, which arrived in March 1988 as 96-99. They had previously been with T. Cowie (Grey Green Coaches) who had purchased them new in 1980/81. They became UD1196-9 and 1196 (FYX 812W) is still in IVL colours when pictured entering Pontypridd bus station on 3 February 1990. It is working the X38 via Nelson, Gelligaer and Bargoed to Phillipstown, New Tredegar. 1196 eventually passed to Phil Anslow Travel after National Welsh went into receivership.

*(the late John Wiltshire)*

In 1987 National Welsh received its last new coaches and to the surprise of many, these were not Leyland Tigers. Delivered as XC965-8 (D625-8 YCX) they were DAF MB230 models with attractive Plaxton Paramount 3500 III 51-seat bodies and the luxury of an integral toilet. The DAF MB230 was a mid-engined coach chassis that first appeared in the United Kingdom in 1975 as the MB200. The Plaxton Paramount 3500 III coach body was launched in 1986 with a revised front end and interior together with bonded glazing. They were delivered in National Express white livery, but by early 1990, XC966 had received the new National Welsh coach livery. This is shown to good effect in this view outside Cardiff Castle on 9 February that year. All four coaches were later re-registered and XC966 became AAX 562A. With the break-up of National Welsh in February 1992, it passed to Tellings Golden Miller and was quickly sold on to Stevenson, Uttoxeter. It later worked for Copelands of Meir near Stoke-on-Trent, as MIB 279, and named Lady Elizabeth III.

*(John Jones)*

The Leyland Olympian was unveiled at the 1980 Commercial Motor Show incorporating many components used in the integral Titan B15. Available as a separate chassis capable of taking both low and normal height bodywork, the Olympian was aimed at a broad market including the National Bus Company. National Welsh initially based five of its ten Olympians at Porth including HR8215 (MUH 289X). They were regular performers on the services from the Rhondda valleys and Pontypridd into Cardiff. HR8215 became HR1859 in 1983 and HR859 in 1986.

This is how we see the bus at Pontypridd on 3 March 1990 in post-deregulation livery. Tellings Golden Miller (TGM) acquired the nine surviving Olympians in February 1992, passing them to the newly-formed Rhondda Buses in May that year. MUH 289X was withdrawn in July 1995 and immediately sold to Armchair, Brentford, but had been sold again by 2000. On 21 June 2011 it was acquired by the Cardiff Transport Preservation Group and fully restored to its original condition as HR8215 in NBC Poppy red livery.

*(the late John Wiltshire)*

In July 1989 AAX 529A, originally SDW 931Y, became the first recipient of "Swiftlink" local coach livery following the removal of its toilet, servery and drinks machine, and conversion into a 53-seater. It was then officially reclassified UD915 though this appears to have been overlooked when applying the finishing touches. The unusual livery seems to suit the Plaxton Paramount body quite well as passengers are picked up at Pontypridd bus station on 31 March 1990 on an X4 working from Cardiff to Abergavenny. One of a batch of twenty similar Leyland Tiger TRCTL11/3R coaches received in 1983 (see also page 55), it was numbered UC1215 before becoming UC215 in 1986 and then UC915 by 1988, to make way for Bustler minibus 215. UD915 passed to Red & White in 1991 and received its red and grey version of "Swiftlink" livery.

*(the late John Wiltshire)*

From 1988, National Welsh vehicles that were operating with Red & White fleet names in the Welsh border areas, began receiving a new livery of red with white and grey stripes and a black skirt. The attractive result is seen to good effect on Leyland National N595 (SKG 905S). This view was taken on 25 April 1990 at Wyesham which is across the River Wye from Monmouth. The Monmouth-bound bus has come up the Wye Valley from Chepstow, passing through historic Tintern along the way. N595 was one of six 11.3 metre Leyland Nationals delivered to Red & White in September 1977 as N31-677 (SKG 904-9S), when N3277 was allocated to Tredegar depot. It passed to National Welsh in 1978 and in 1983 it became N1595 and then N595 in 1986. N595 passed into Western Travel Ltd ownership in 1991 together with the eastern area operations.

*(John Jones)*

In 1983/84 Rhymney Valley District Council received three East Lancs-bodied Leyland Tiger saloons numbered 71-73. Of these 71 (A71 VTX) was a very rare 10-metre version with 43 dual-purpose seats, while 72/3 (A72/3 VTX) were the 11-metre model and featured 47 similar seats. In August 1984 a further three similar 11-metre Tigers were delivered and entered service as 25-7 (B25-7 ADW), joining 72/3 at Caerphilly depot. All passed to Inter Valley Link in 1986 and the longer Tigers were included in the National Welsh takeover in April 1989, but were immediately put up for sale. Having failed to attract buyers, they became National Welsh UD695-9 (B25-7 ADW, A72/3 VTX) respectively. Between April and June 1990 they were repainted into Caerphilly Buslink livery and based at the new Bedwas depot. Having just re-entered service, U696 is caught leaving Bargoed on 28 April 1990 on its long run from Merthyr Tydfil to Newport. In 1992 all five Tigers passed to Rhondda Buses Ltd where they gave several more years' service.

*(John Jones)*

South Wales Transport received its first Bristol VRTs in late 1976 some nine months before the Western Welsh group of companies. Fitted with ECW 74-seat bodies and Leyland 501 engines, South Wales Transport numbered them 905-16 (OCY 905-16R). In 1987, OCY 911-3R were transferred to National Welsh where they became HR824-6. On 29 May 1990, we are in Frogmore Street, Abergavenny, as HR824 (OCY 911R) is busy on a town service. This bus is in a variation of the new National Welsh livery, including a white lower front panel and grille. HR824 was amongst the vehicles which passed to Western Travel in February 1991, while HR825/6 remained with National Welsh.

*(John Jones)*

In 1987 Caerphilly was a hotbed of competition amongst bus operators and, in response to this, National Welsh created its Caerphilly Buslink operation with its own distinctive red and yellow livery. It had been sharing a yard at Bedwas with Waddon's Coaches, until the site was acquired in November 1988 for its Caerphilly Buslink operation. The allocation included just one double-decker, a VRT, and a number of Leyland Nationals. NS473 (YBO 148T) is a typical example of a Caerphilly Buslink Leyland National, and is a 10.3-metre model that was new in February 1979 as NS1579. It is seen in Bridge Street, Pontypridd, on 25 July 1990 as it approaches the A470 junction and was still owned by National Welsh in early 1992.

*(Geoff Gould)*

As we have already seen, in December 1987 National Welsh adopted a new red, white and green livery with a bilingual fleet name and incorporating a red dragon. This was applied to single and double-deck buses, together with a variation for dual-purpose vehicles. Minibuses continued to carry the well-established yellow Bustler livery. HR830 (GHB 86W) is picking up customers at Pontypridd bus station on a gloomy 1 December 1990, before heading off to Maerdy. HR830 is one of three Bristol VRTs with East Lancs 76-seat bodywork that National Welsh acquired with the Inter Valley Link fleet in April 1989, all three including HR828/9 (GHB 84/5W) now allocated to the Porth depot. These buses passed to a series of dealers before ending up with Constable Coaches (Beeston's) of Long Melford, Suffolk, in September 1992. GHB 86W was retained by them as a school bus until 1995 when it was sold to Day and Ellwood of Chatteris, and re-registered PIL 6950.

*(Andrew Wiltshire)*

Now in the new livery, 429 (NWO 463R) is seen arriving at Maesteg on 1 March 1991 working from Bridgend to Glyncorrwg, over in the Afan valley. It was new as Western Welsh ND1876 in March 1977, one of a batch of ten 11.3-metre Leyland Nationals fitted with 48 dual-purpose seats. After passing to National Welsh in 1978, it was renumbered ND1429 in 1983, shortened to ND429 in 1986, and the prefix was eventually dropped. NWO 463R later passed to London & Country (Guildford & West Surrey) and was rebuilt by British Bus receiving a Cummins B series engine and Allison gearbox. Plaxton Paramount parts were used to modify the front dash and the interior was re-trimmed. It passed to Colchester Borough Transport in 1996 as LNC463 and to Arriva, Colchester, two years later. NWO 463R was later working for Cheney Travel, Banbury, and was noted in 2004 with registration KUI 5159.

(John Jones)

In 1991 National Welsh began repainting vehicles into a maroon and white livery which would be quicker and hence cheaper to apply than the livery shown on the previous page. This is shown here on ECW-bodied Bristol VRT 708 (BUH 233V), one of five VRTs that National Welsh had converted to dual-purpose layout by fitting 67 high-backed seats, which has yet to receive any fleet names. It is seen descending The Walk at Merthyr Tydfil on 27 April 1991, returning to the town centre from the Prince Charles Hospital at Gurnos. 1991 was to be another difficult year for National Welsh but a few buses did eventually receive this livery. The substantial Merthyr Tydfil operations dated from June 1989 and hastened the demise of the incumbent operator, Merthyr Tydfil Transport. It was amongst several operating areas which passed to a consortium of Drawlane, Stevensons (SBS) and Tellings Golden Miller (TGM) on 4 February. The Merthyr operation, including this bus, was then sold on to Offerdemo Ltd (Cynon Valley Transport Ltd), and renamed Merthyr Bus.

*(John Jones)*

This view was taken at the South Road bus stand in Porthcawl on 5 September 1991 and sadly shows a somewhat shabby side of the National Welsh fleet by this time. Leyland National NS476 (YDW 398T) is still in NBC poppy red livery, but has been adorned with the latest National Welsh fleet names, plus a Rhondda vinyl to emphasise its local credentials for good measure. The careworn state of the advert adds to the rather untidy appearance. NS476 is now based at Porth depot and has worked into Porthcawl from Pontypridd via Talbot Green, Llanharry and Bridgend. It was new to National Welsh as NS1879, and entered service in February 1979 along with NS11-779 (YBO 144-50T). NS476 passed to Rhondda Bus in 1992 and gained a simple but attractive maroon and cream livery.

*(John Jones)*

As we have seen on page 64, the former Inter Valley Link MCW Metroriders acquired by National Welsh duly entered service as 2101-17 based at Merthyr Tydfil depot and received Bustler livery in due course. In February 1991 three of them, 2101/5/10, went on loan to Red & White at Cwmbran. Later that year 2105 (F105 YWO) was allocated to a special rail-link service in the Rhondda Fawr which was sponsored by Mid Glamorgan County Council. On 5 September 1991, 2105 is photographed heading away from Treherbert station along Station Street, and about to cross the Rhondda River on service VL1 to Blaenrhondda. Its attractive silver, blue and white livery features the slogan "I meet the train". All seventeen Metroriders passed to Rhondda Buses Ltd in May 1992 and a number of them were later engaged on rail-link services from stations at Maesteg, Tondu and Pontyclun. 2105 was still working for Rhondda in 1998 in Caerphilly Busways livery.

*(John Jones)*

On 3 January 1992 National Welsh went into official receivership followed by the sale of the Aberdare, Merthyr and Porth operations on 4 February and the closure of the Bridgend depot on 16 February. What remained of National Welsh was left to linger at Barry where Cardiff Bus had intensified competition in the company's last stronghold. An employee buy-out was agreed in May 1992, which would trade as Barry Bus-Line and Bustler. Ten used Ford Transits were quickly acquired to replace the original Transits which had passed to Rhondda Buses in the Drawlane, SBS and TGM deal in February. One of these is 431 (C352 GFJ) a Robin Hood-bodied example, which began life with North Devon in 1986. It is seen in Tynewydd Road, Barry, on 8 May 1992 on a local service to Highlight Park. It had only recently entered service and is in a simplified version of the original Bustler livery.

*(the late John Wiltshire)*

One of the double-deckers still running out of Barry depot in the Barry Bus-Line era was HR832 (WTU 474W), one of a pair of Bristol VRTs received in 1990 from Crosville Wales in exchange for the two convertible open-toppers (page 66). HR832 and sister bus HR831 (WTU 473W) differed from all other National Welsh ECW-bodied VRTs as they were Gardner 6LXB-powered which gave them a more business-like exhaust note. HR832 is also seen on Tynewydd Road in Barry on 8 May 1992, operating a Tesco shopper service. Due to the intensive competition in the Barry area, Broad Street bus depot at Barry closed its doors for the last time on the evening of 7 August 1992. After just 14 years in existence, National Welsh was officially laid to rest. The final fleet had comprised 13 double-deckers, six saloons and 25 minibuses.

*(the late John Wiltshire)*